Engineers
Build
Models

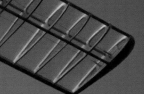

Reagan Miller

Crabtree Publishing Company
www.crabtreebooks.com

Author
Reagan Miller

Publishing plan research and development:
Reagan Miller

Editor
Crystal Sikkens

Proofreader
Shannon Welbourn

Design
Samara Parent

Photo research
Reagan Miller
Crystal Sikkens

**Production coordinator
and prepress technician**
Samara Parent

Print coordinator
Margaret Amy Salter

Photographs
© Roger Ressmeyer/CORBIS: page 19
Dreamstime: cover (right)
iStockphoto: page 11 (left inset)
Shutterstock: oconnelll: page 18
Thinkstock: page 14 (left)
All other images by Shutterstock

Library and Archives Canada Cataloguing in Publication

Miller, Reagan, author
    Engineers build models / Reagan Miller.

(Engineering close-up)
Includes index.
Issued in print and electronic formats.
ISBN 978-0-7787-0093-7 (bound).--ISBN 978-0-7787-0100-2 (pbk.).--
ISBN 978-1-4271-9404-6 (pdf).--ISBN 978-1-4271-9400-8 (html)

    1. Models and modelmaking--Juvenile literature. 2. Engineers--
Juvenile literature. I. Title.

TA154.M55 2013   j688.1   C2013-906286-6
                                          C2013-906287-4

Library of Congress Cataloging-in-Publication Data

Miller, Reagan, author.
    Engineers build models / Reagan Miller.
      pages cm. -- (Engineering close-up)
    Includes index.
    ISBN 978-0-7787-0093-7 (reinforced library binding : alk. paper) -- ISBN 978-
0-7787-0100-2 (pbk. : alk. paper) --ISBN 978-1-4271-9404-6 (electronic pdf) --
ISBN 978-1-4271-9400-8 (electronic html)
    1. Engineering models--Juvenile literature. 2. Models and modelmaking--
Juvenile literature. 3. Engineering--Juvenile literature. I. Title.
  TA177.M55 2014
  620.001'1--dc23
                          2013050336

Crabtree Publishing Company

www.crabtreebooks.com   1-800-387-7650

Printed in Canada/032014/MA20140124

Published in Canada
Crabtree Publishing
616 Welland Ave.
St. Catharines, Ontario
L2M 5V6

Published in the United States
Crabtree Publishing
PMB 59051
350 Fifth Avenue, 59th Floor
New York, New York 10118

Published in the United Kingdom
Crabtree Publishing
Maritime House
Basin Road North, Hove
BN41 1WR

Published in Australia
Crabtree Publishing
3 Charles Street
Coburg North
VIC 3058

Contents

Who designs our world?

Have you ever looked up at a **skyscraper** or down at your running shoes and wondered how these things were made? They were first created by **engineers**! Engineers are the people who **design** many of the things in our world. To design means to make a plan to do or build something that solves a problem.

skyscraper

running shoes

4

Engineers design technologies

The things engineers design are called **technologies**. A technology is anything people make that solves a problem or meets a need. For example, a car is a technology that meets people's need to get from place to place quickly.

Technology is all around us! An umbrella is a technology because it solves the problem of getting wet when it is raining outside.

5

Technologies take time

Engineers have important jobs. They use math, science, and **creative thinking** to design technologies. Long before people use a technology, such as a bridge, engineers have spent a lot of time designing it to make sure it works well and is safe.

Engineers spent more than 65 years designing the Golden Gate bridge in San Francisco, California, before building began!

Working together

Engineers often work together in groups to design technologies. Working in groups lets engineers share different ideas. Engineers **communicate** their ideas to the people they work with and other people outside of the group. To communicate means to write, speak, or draw to share information.

What do you **think?**

What are some ways you can communicate your ideas to people?

What is a model?

One way engineers communicate their ideas to others is by making **models**. A model is a **representation** of a real object. A model can show how different parts of an object work together. A model can also show how something looks.

This boy has made a model of an airplane. The model helps him learn how the parts of an airplane work together.

Map models

This map is a model of a garden. It gives us information about where different fruits and vegetables are planted. The map is a model because it helps us understand more about how the real garden looks.

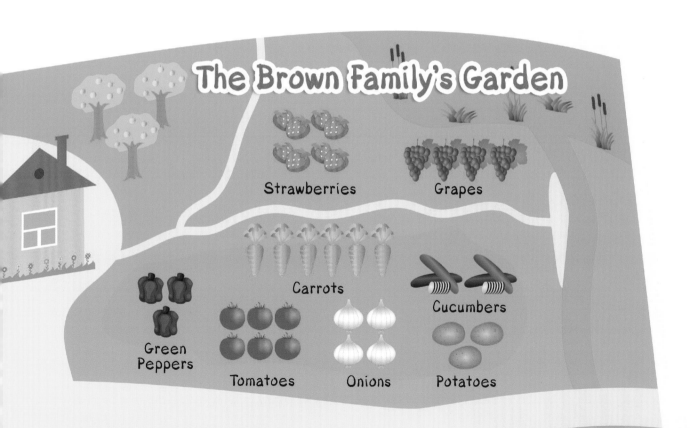

The Brown Family's Garden

Strawberries

Grapes

Carrots

Cucumbers

Green Peppers

Tomatoes

Onions

Potatoes

Models are not exactly like the things they represent. For example, some models may not have all of the same parts or **features** as the real thing. A toy car is a model of a real car. It has four tires and can move forward and backward, but it is much smaller and cannot move as fast as a real car.

Could you get a ride to school in a toy car?

Different parts

Models can be used to show things that are very large and have many different parts, such as a **wind turbine**. Building a real wind turbine would take a lot of time and cost a lot of money. A model turbine takes less time to build and shows how the different parts fit and work together.

blades

blades

The **blades** on this boy's model of a wind turbine spin like the blades on a real turbine.

Diagrams and blueprints

Some models are drawn on paper or made using a computer. A **diagram** is a drawing that shows the parts of an object and how it works. A diagram has labels. Labels are words that name or describe the different parts and help others understand the model better.

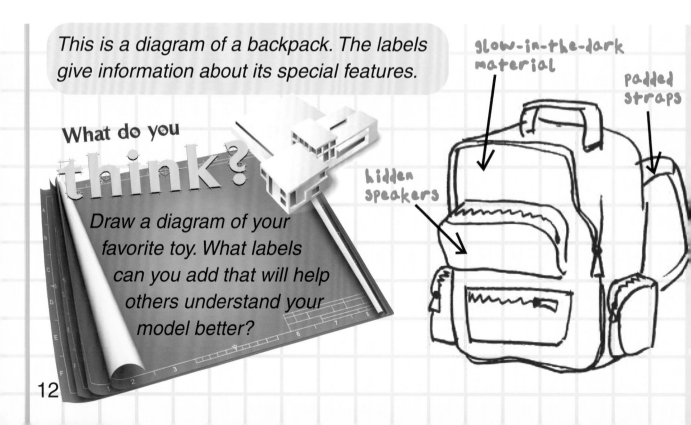

This is a diagram of a backpack. The labels give information about its special features.

glow-in-the-dark material

padded straps

hidden speakers

What do you think?

Draw a diagram of your favorite toy. What labels can you add that will help others understand your model better?

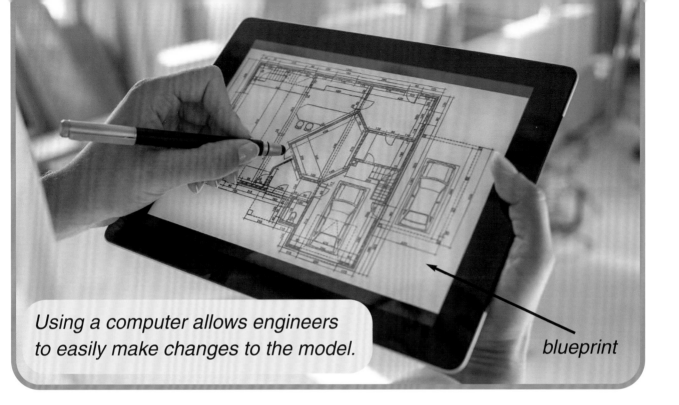

Using a computer allows engineers to easily make changes to the model.

blueprint

Blueprints

A **blueprint** is another kind of model that engineers use to show their design ideas to others. Blueprints are drawings that show the different parts of a building. For example, a blueprint for a school shows where the classrooms will be built. Engineers can draw blueprints on paper or using a computer.

Different forms

Models have different forms. For example, a map of the world and a globe are both models of Earth. Maps are flat, or **two-dimensional** models. They show length and width. A globe is a solid object. It is **three-dimensional.**

map

globe

3-D models

Three-dimensional models have length, width, and height. You can hold a three-dimensional model and look at it from above, below, and all sides. These kinds of models are also called 3-D models.

What do you think?

Give one example of another two-dimensional model and another three-dimensional model.

*A **diorama** is a kind of 3-D model. This diorama is a model of a house.*

How models are helpful

Models are helpful in many ways. Engineers make models to explain, or help people understand, their ideas for solving problems. People can review the model and give **feedback**, or suggestions, to the engineer to help make the design idea better.

This engineer is using a model to explain his idea to his team.

A designer, not a builder

Engineers do not make or build the things they design. The engineer can use their model to explain to the people who are building it how to build it properly. Engineers may visit the site where it is being built to make sure it is done correctly and answer any questions.

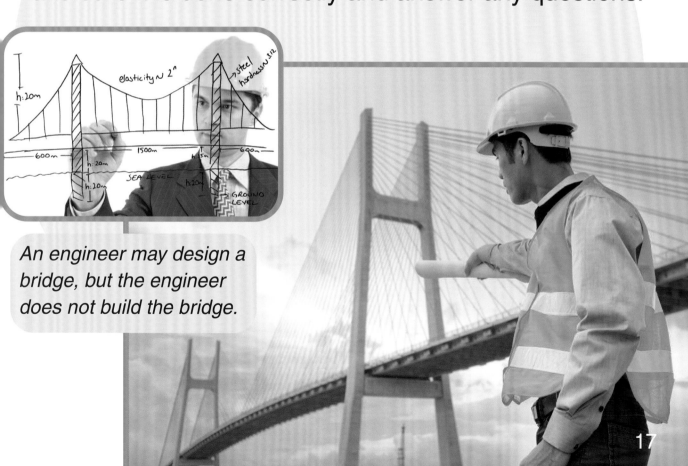

An engineer may design a bridge, but the engineer does not build the bridge.

Testing, testing

Engineers also build models to test their design ideas. Testing models helps engineers know if their ideas will work and are safe. They can also find out what changes they need to make to the model to make it better.

These students have made model cars. They are testing them to see which one will run the farthest using power from the Sun.

Shake tables move the same way as an earthquake. This allows the engineer to see the damage a home would receive in an earthquake.

shake table

Earthquake!

Earthquakes cause the ground to shake. They happen in many areas of the world. Engineers try to design houses that will receive the least amount of damage from shaking. Models of houses are tested on special tables called shake tables to see which designs work the best.

Engineers plan

Before making a model, engineers first make a plan. A good plan is important because it helps the engineer figure out how to make their model. **Materials** are an important part when planning a model. Materials are what objects are made of. Different materials have different **properties**. Properties describe how something looks, feels, or acts.

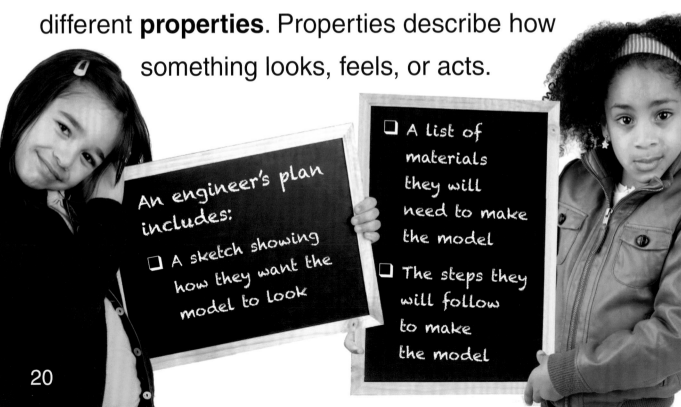

An engineer's plan includes:

☐ A sketch showing how they want the model to look

☐ A list of materials they will need to make the model

☐ The steps they will follow to make the model

Materials matter!

Choosing the best materials is an important part of building models. Some materials are better than others for making certain things. Would you wear rain boots made of cardboard? Of course not! Cardboard would let in water and make your feet wet. Rubber is a better material. Rubber is waterproof. It does not let water pass through.

A kite is made to fly in the air. To design a kite, an engineer would choose a material that is light so the kite can stay up in the air.

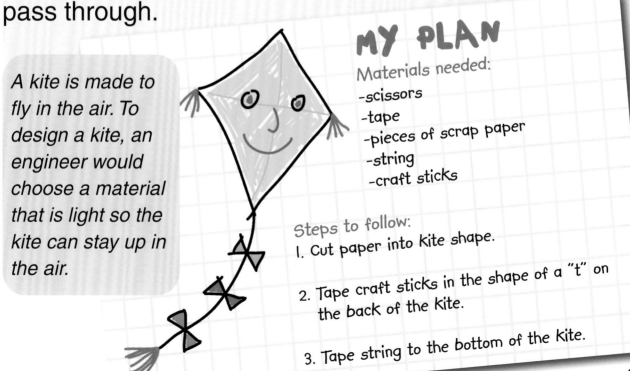

MY PLAN

Materials needed:
-scissors
-tape
-pieces of scrap paper
-string
-craft sticks

Steps to follow:
1. Cut paper into kite shape.

2. Tape craft sticks in the shape of a "t" on the back of the kite.

3. Tape string to the bottom of the kite.

Flying high!

In 1903, the Wright brothers made history when they became the first people to fly in an airplane. They spent more than four years building and testing thousands of different models.

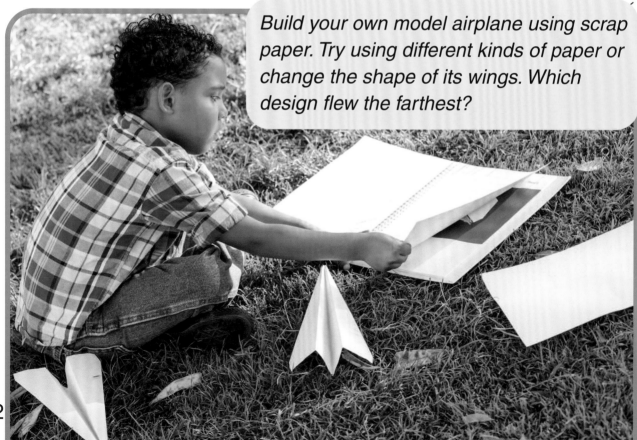

Build your own model airplane using scrap paper. Try using different kinds of paper or change the shape of its wings. Which design flew the farthest?

Learning more

Books

The Three Little Pigs: An Architectural Tale. by Steven Guarnaccia.
    Abrams Books for Young Readers, 2010.

Build It! Invent New Structures and Contraptions (Fact Finders)
    by Tammy Enz. Capstone Press, 2012.

Websites

This website offers creative engineering challenges and the latest engineering news for kids.
www.inventivekids.com

This website features interactive labs that explore forces, motion, and shapes.
Building Big: The Labs:
pbs.org/wgbh/buildingbig/lab/index.html

Words to know

Note: Some bolded words are defined in the text

blades (bleyds) noun The turning part on a wind turbine. A blade looks like an airplane propeller.

creative thinking (KREE-ey-tiv thing-king) noun Being able to use your mind to create new and original ideas

features (FEE-cher) noun A part or detail of something that stands out

representation (rep-ri-zen-TA-shuhn) noun Something that stands in place of another thing with similar features

skyscraper (SKAHY-skrey-per) noun A very tall building

wind turbine (wind TUR-bin) noun A windmill that changes wind energy into electricity

A noun is a person, place, or thing.

Index